EDWARD HOPPER

EDWARD HOPPER

Maria Costantino

Grange
BOOKS

Published by Grange Books
An imprint of Grange Books PLC
The Grange
Grange Yard
London SE1 3AG

Produced by Saturn Books
Kiln House, 210 New Kings Road
London SW6 4NZ

ISBN 1 85627 972 3

Printed in China

Reprinted 1996

PAGE 1: The artist,
Edward Hopper.

PAGE 2: **Compartment C,
Car 293** (Detail), 1938
Oil on canvas, 20 × 19 in.
Collection of I.B.M.
Corporation, Armonk, NY

BELOW: **Room in New York,**
1932
Oil on canvas, 29 × 36 in.
UNL – F. M. Hall Collection,
Sheldon Memorial Art Gallery,
University of Nebraska,
Lincoln, NE
(1936.H-166)

CONTENTS

INTRODUCTION

One of the giants of American art, and generally considered the major twentieth-century realist, Edward Hopper was born in the small Hudson River town of Nyack, New York, on 22 July 1882, the second and last child of Elizabeth Griffith Smith and Garrett Henry Hopper. A solidly middle-class family, the Hoppers owned and ran a dry-goods store and attended the local Baptist church which had been founded by Elizabeth's grandfather in the early nineteenth century. The Hoppers' home was only a block away from the Hudson River, and at the time of Hopper's childhood Nyack was a busy port town with a thriving shipyard that specialized in building racing yachts. An early fascination with the river and boats no doubt encouraged the young Hopper to consider a career as a naval architect at one time, as well as providing him with the theme for many of his paintings in later life. Hopper was drawn not only to sailing boats, but to every type of seagoing vessel – including tramp steamers and trawlers – and some of his most successful watercolors depict such nautical themes:

Gloucester Harbor (1926), *The Dory* (1925), and *Yawl Riding a Swell* (1935) are but three of such works.

Hopper's, and also his older sister Marion's, interest in art had been encouraged from an early age by their mother, and by the age of 10 Eddie, as he was called, was already sufficiently confident of his work to sign and date his drawings. By the time Hopper graduated from Nyack High School he was intent on becoming an artist. His parents, however, were concerned that their son should plan for a secure income, and persuaded him to study commercial art. In 1899 Hopper therefore began the daily commuter's journey from Nyack to New York City to study at the Correspondence School of Illustrating at 114 West 34th Street. A year later, however, Hopper was to transfer to the New York School of Art, popularly known as the "Chase School," after its best-known teacher, William Merritt Chase. Chase, along with the other members of the faculty (in particular Robert Henri and Kenneth Hayes Miller, who were to be Hopper's most important teachers), encouraged the students to

Along the River Front, Nyack, N.Y.

RIGHT: Manet's masterpiece, *Olympia*, from which Hopper drew his inspiration.

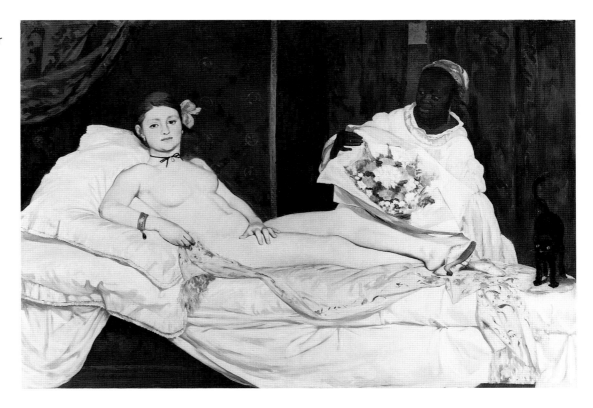

visit the Metropolitan Museum of Art and to study the artists of the past, especially Rembrandt, Goya, and the modern masters Manet, Degas and Daumier. The influence of the modern masters of French painting is evident in many of Hopper's works from this time: as well as making drawings after Manet's *The Fifer* and *Olympia*, Hopper's early style, with its use of large areas of shadow and rubbed backgrounds, recalls drawings by Millet and Seurat, whose works he may well have known in reproduction.

LEFT: A hand-tinted postcard showing the view along the river front at Nyack, N.Y., Hopper's home town.

RIGHT: William Merritt Chase instructing his students in the Shinnecock Hills, *c.* 1901. Such was Chase's renown, that the New York School of Art, which numbered Hopper among its students, became known as the ''Chase School.''

At the New York School of Art Hopper's talent was recognized with prizes and scholarships, and later with the opportunity to teach Saturday classes in life drawing, painting and composition. In 1904 one of Hopper's sketches of a woman holding an umbrella was among the student works to be selected for reproduction in an article about the school published in the magazine *The Sketch Book*. Unfortunately, a misprint meant that the sketch was credited to an "Edward Hoppen."

By 1906, Hopper, encouraged by his teachers, began to feel that it was time to travel to Europe to see at first hand the works of the great masters that he had for so long admired and studied. By this time he was already employed by the New York advertising agency C. C. Phillips and Company, where he worked part-time as an illustrator. Yet Hopper was restless, and realized that he would never find total satisfaction in illustration work. In October 1906, therefore, with the financial help of his parents, Hopper left for the artistic capital of the world at that time – Paris – where he would stay for nearly eight months. Through contacts in the Nyack Baptist church, it was arranged for Hopper to lodge with a French family – a widow and her two teenaged sons – in a building in the rue de Lille owned by the Eglise Evangelique Baptiste.

ABOVE: *The Railroad* – Hopper's depiction of a French railroad-station scene.

LEFT: Hopper's brooding work, *The Dome*, is similar in atmosphere to Meryon's *L'Abside de Nôtre Dame*.

According to Hopper, from his new home he needed only to walk a few yards before he could see both the Louvre museum and the Sacre Cœur.

At first in Paris Hopper's work wavered between illustration and fine art: as well as making watercolors of French characters — some of which border on the caricature and demonstrate (despite a widespread belief to the contrary) Hopper's keen sense of humor — he also produced drawings that reveal his studies of the French artists Manet and Forain. Instead of enrolling in an art school, Hopper chose to visit exhibitions on his own, and hoped to paint outdoors in and around Paris. During his first few months in the city, however, the weather was wintry and, as a result, Hopper's initial city scenes are dark in tone and generally restricted to views of his building with its interior courtyard.

In spring, when the weather broke, Hopper began to paint outside along the banks of the River Seine, often taking a boat to nearby St.-Cloud or Charenton. By this time it is evident that Hopper had learned much from seeing the works of the Impressionists at first hand. While his early Paris works were dark and somber in tone and were painted with smooth, unbroken brushstrokes, his later paintings of 1907, like *Après-Midi de Juin*, *Tugboat at Boulevard Saint Michel*, and *Le Louvre et la Seine*, display brushstrokes that are shorter and more fragmented, and his palette is lighter, its pastel colors reminiscent of the Impressionists. Yet Hopper was later to deny the impact of the Impressionists on his work, although in his letters home he did admit to seeing their works, and was especially impressed by the paintings of Sisley, Renoir, Pissarro and Monet.

In June 1907 Hopper left Paris for London, where he visited the galleries, museums and cathedrals. In his letters home he said that he found London less beautiful than Paris, and decided to return to France via Amsterdam and Haarlem in the Netherlands. At the Rijksmuseum in Amsterdam, Hopper saw Rembrandt's *The Nightwatch*, which he described as the most wonderful painting he had ever seen. In Haarlem he saw the works of Frans Hals, and met up with his former teacher, Robert Henri, who was conducting a summer school there for American students. Brief visits to Berlin and Brussels followed, before Hopper arrived back in Paris for a three-week stay. Then, on 21 August 1907, Hopper sailed home to New York, where he began work as an illustrator, employed by the Sherman and Bryan advertising agency.

Hopper's first chance to show his works in public came the following year, in 1908, when a group exhibition organized by several former students of the Chase School was staged as a protest against the conservative tastes of the selecting juries at the National Academy. At the "Exhibition of Paintings and Drawings by Contemporary American Artists" Hopper showed three oils: *Le Louvre et la Seine*, *The Bridge of the Arts*, and *The Park at St.-Cloud*, as well as a drawing. Except for Hopper and Guy Pere du Bois, who also showed a Parisian scene, all the other artists exhibited paintings of American subjects. But while the reviewer for the *New York American* magazine praised the exhibition and hailed it as a step toward a truly "national" art (despite, it seems, the inclusion of French subjects), on the whole the exhibition was ignored by both the art establishment and most of New York's other critics.

Once back in America, Hopper continued to paint: his 1908 works included several reminiscences of France, such as *Valley of the Seine*, as well as New York scenes like *The El Station*, and *Railroad Train*, which were probably inspired by his own daily journey from Nyack to New York.

In March 1909 Hopper returned to Paris, resuming his painting along the banks of the Seine and making excursions to paint at Chartres, Fontainebleau and St.-

ABOVE: John Sloan – a leading light of the "Ash Can School."

LEFT: Hopper's 1921 etching, *Evening Wind*.

BELOW: *Gloucester Harbor*, painted by Hopper in 1912.

One of the most outstanding of Hopper's paintings from 1909, although it was most probably painted when he returned to America, points the way toward Hopper's future interest in depicting the solitary female nude posed in an interior, alongside the exploration of the interior space itself. *Summer Interior* (1909), with its broad areas of solid color, and its calm, contemplative mood, also recalls the theme of paintings by Degas.

Characteristically, the solitary figures which inhabit Hopper's paintings appear to be lost in thought. Sometimes the figure is shown at work, like the man raking leaves in *Pennsylvania Coal Town* (1947); at other times the figure is engrossed in reading, like the manicurist in *Barber Shop* (1931). Often the figures are just waiting, as in *Sunday* (1926), *French Six-day Bicycle Rider* (1937), or *Summertime* (1943). And even when there are other figures visible in the painting, the central characters appear to inhabit their own private space. Among Hopper's several paintings of solitary figures are those of women, often nude or in a state of undress: *Eleven A.M.* (1926), *Morning in a City* (1944), *High Noon* (1949), and *Morning Sun* (1952), are all examples. These later paintings are also concerned with the symbolism of the "time of day," an interpretation supported by Hopper's fondness for the work of certain poets, in particular Verlaine, Goethe and Frost. This interest in "times of day" may have come about following Hopper's

Germain-en-Laye. But the unusually heavy rain throughout his stay made him cut his visit short, and at the end of July he sailed home.

introduction to the French Symbolist poets during his student days in Robert Henri's classes. Furthermore, the works of the Symbolist poets, composers, and painters were still fashionable in Paris when Hopper first arrived there in 1906. In his paintings of evening time, Hopper often conveyed a sense of mystery, such as in *House at Dusk* (1935), *Shakespear at Dusk* (1935), and *Cape Cod Evening* (1939). Hopper was equally fascinated by night-time, and used the theme in a number of works, ranging from etchings like *Night on the El Train* (1918), to his later oil paintings, *Night Windows* (1928), *Office at Night* (1940), and *Nighthawks* (1942).

Hopper made his last trip abroad in May 1910, when he stayed in Paris for a few weeks before embarking on a long-planned trip to Spain. Back in New York, he continued to paint reminiscences of France, like *Le Bistro or The Wine Shop*, and had a second opportunity to show his works, at the Exhibition of Independent Artists organized by John Sloan and Robert Henri in April 1910. Here Hopper showed only one painting – *The Louvre* – which did not sell, nor did it receive any mention in the press. But Hopper's participation in the show was nevertheless important, as it identified him as one of the leading independent young artists of a new American art movement.

Hopper next took part in a group exhibition held at the MacDowell Club in February and March 1912, where he showed five oils, four of which were unambiguously French themes, while the fifth painting – *Sailing* – was of an American scene. Once again, however, none of his paintings sold.

That summer Hopper went to Gloucester, Massachusetts, to paint with Leon Kroll, a former student at the Art Students' League and the National Academy. At Gloucester Hopper focused his attention on painting the picturesque waterfront and rocky shoreline of the area. No doubt he was attracted to the harbor, which was full of boats, but he also found here the intense sunlight that he now preferred. Later, in 1923, when Hopper returned to Gloucester, he would begin working in a new medium – watercolor – in which he almost invariably avoided including any figures, concentrating instead on the local architecture and on capturing the qualities of the light.

In February 1913 Hopper again showed *Sailing* in the International Exhibition of Modern Art in New York, the exhibition more commonly known as the Armory Show. The avant-garde European art on show attracted enormous attention and critical acclaim, and Hopper's painting sold for $250. This was his first sale, but it did not lead directly to the sale of other works, and for the next decade Hopper was to struggle financially.

Since 1912 Hopper had been producing illustrations for several periodicals, including *Sunday Magazine*, *The Metropolitan Magazine*, *Everybody's*, and *System, The Magazine of Business*. While he found working as an illustrator depressing and restricting, it was his only source of income. Nevertheless, Hopper refused to work as an illustrator for more than three days a week, preferring to trade a restricted income for the free time to paint.

At the end of 1913 Hopper moved his New York studio to 3 Washington Square North, where, as and when his financial situation allowed, he gradually rented additional space, and where he would live for the rest of life.

Two further group shows at the MacDowell Club followed in 1914, and during that summer Hopper painted in Ogunquit, Maine, where he studied the coastline and local architecture. But it was 1915 that would mark the first turning point in Hopper's career:

LEFT: A view of Monhegan Island, whose rugged beauty captivated Hopper in 1916.

OPPOSITE PAGE: Jo, Hopper's wife, as sketched by him between 1935 and 1940.

firstly, he was introduced by a fellow student, Martin Lewis, to the techniques of etching; and, secondly, at a group show at the MacDowell Club, two of Hopper's paintings – *Soir Bleu* (1914), and *New York Corner* (1913), were singled out by the critics for discussion, though *Soir Bleu* was condemned as an "ambitious fantasy." Despite such negative reactions, Hopper still remained closely involved with French imagery, but he would never again exhibit the monumental painting of a French café scene, whose elements appear to have been inspired by Watteau's *Gilles* (the clown dressed in white), and Toulouse-Lautrec's *At the Moulin Rouge* (the standing woman with a heavily painted face). When Hopper next showed at the MacDowell Club, in November 1915, he showed *American Village* (1912), *Rocks and Houses*, and *The Dories, Ogunquit* (both 1914): three oils depicting American scenes, the last two painted at Ogunquit.

In the summer of 1916 Hopper went to Monhegan Island in Maine, where he again worked outside on paintings of the rugged coastline. So captivated was he by the beauty of the island, that Hopper was to return there for the next few summers. While his paintings still received little critical attention, Hopper's reputation as a commercial illustrator was flourishing, and he was now contributing regularly to the *Farmer's Wife* and *Country Gentleman* magazines, as well as producing cover illustrations for the *Wells Fargo Messenger*.

In October 1918 Hopper won his first award since art school, for a four-color poster entitled *Smash The Hun*. Ironically, the award brought Hopper more publicity and critical attention than he had ever known, and lifted him out of artistic obscurity. In January 1920, at the age of 37, Hopper finally had his first one-man show of paintings at the Whitney Studio Club. Of the 16 oils on show, 11 had been painted in France over a decade earlier, while the remainder were of American scenes painted in Massachusetts or Maine. However, none of the paintings were sold.

In the summer of 1923 Hopper returned to Gloucester, where he began working in watercolors, his first real use of the medium since his school days. It is possible that he was encouraged to experiment in this medium by Jo Nivison. Hopper and Nivison had both been students at the Chase School, and had met again by chance during the summers when Hopper was at Ogunquit and Monhegan Island. Jo had already exhibited her own watercolors when the Brooklyn Museum invited her to show in a group exhibition in late 1923. It was Jo who suggested that Hopper submit his watercolors for the same show. Six of Hopper's paintings were selected for exhibition and were hung alongside Nivison's. Jo's gesture in bringing Hopper's work to the attention of the museum proved significant: while the critics were to ignore her work, they raved about Hopper's and, in December 1923, the Brooklyn Museum purchased *The*

Mansard Roof for $100 – Hopper's first sale since the Armory Show in 1913.

Shortly before his forty-second birthday, on 9 July 1924, Hopper and Jo were married. That summer, spent at Gloucester, Hopper produced a number of watercolors which were shown in his second one-man show, this time at the commercial Frank K. M. Rehn Gallery. All 11 watercolors, plus five additional paintings, were sold, and the exhibition proved to be the major turning point in Hopper's career: he was now finally able to give up his work as a commercial illustrator and devote himself entirely to his painting.

Although their personalities were very different, Hopper and Jo shared many interests: both were well read, both shared a love of poetry and the theater – Jo had been a professional actress for a time – and both had traveled in Europe. Earlier in 1923 Hopper had begun to take evening classes at the Whitney Studio Club where, for 25 cents, he could sketch from the life model. Soon after their marriage, however, Jo insisted that she alone should pose for him, and for the rest of Hopper's life, Jo was the only model for all of his female figures.

In addition to the rural coastlines of New England, Hopper often found inspiration for his paintings in New York City, as can be seen in *Blackwell's Island* (1911), *Queensboro Bridge* (1913), *New York Corner* (1913), *Drug Store* (1927), and *Manhattan Bridge Loop* (1928). As part of his observations of city life, Hopper investigated the office setting for some of his paintings. As an illustrator, he had often depicted office scenes,

particularly for *System* magazine, and these illustrations frequently reveal a close relationship to his paintings. In *Office at Night* (1940), however, Hopper turned once again to the French masters for inspiration, drawing on Degas's *The Cotton Exchange, New Orleans* (1873), one of the few paintings of an office interior. Like Degas, in *Office at Night*, Hopper makes use of a high, oblique view of the floor, and a steeply angled glass wall on the left-hand side. In Hopper's other paintings of city life, such as *New York Movie* (1939), and *Office in a Small City* (1953), his reputation as a painter of loneliness, isolation, and estrangement was confirmed.

Hopper was often restless and unable to paint, and one way of dealing with this situation was to travel with Jo: together they visited Mexico several times and traveled extensively in New England. Along the way Hopper painted, concentrating on the environment inhabited by travelers: hotel lobbies, motel bedrooms, trains, highways and gas stations. Trains, in fact, had attracted Hopper since his childhood, and he had explored the theme of railroads and stations whilst in Paris. Railroad tracks also seem to have had a particular symbolic significance to Hopper: in *Approaching a City* (1946), *House by a Railroad* (1925), and *New York, New Haven and Hartford* (1931), the railroad tracks seem to suggest the movement of modern life in America. In several illustrations and etchings Hopper had also explored the theme of the interiors of trains, a theme to which he would return in *Compartment C, Car 293* (1938), and *Chair Car* (1965); in both paintings women are depicted engrossed in their reading.

Hopper also found inspiration in hotel lobbies and travelers' bedrooms. The first of his paintings on this theme was *Hotel Room* (1931), in which a solitary woman sits on a bed intently reading a letter. Hopper's interest in the psychology of his figures is apparent in *Hotel Lobby* (1943), and *Hotel by a Railroad* (1952). As his mature style emerged, Hopper also developed several compositional formats, which he used frequently throughout his career. These included the frontal view parallel with the picture plane, a scene viewed at an angle from above, and views through a window into interior and exterior spaces. For Hopper, the window motif appears to have been a symbol for the "world beyond," as well as a physical barrier that separates the viewer from the drama taking place beyond it. In *Hotel by a Railroad*, the man gazes out of the window onto the railroad tracks, while in *Hotel Window* (1956) there is a sense of a similar longing for places beyond the window.

LEFT: Degas's painting *The Cotton Exchange, New Orleans* (1873) was especially valued by Hopper, as it was one of the few paintings that portrayed office life.

LEFT: Hopper's watercolor study of Monterrey Cathedral, painted while he was traveling with Jo.

RIGHT: Hopper with his painting *California Hills*, for which he won first place in the Hallmark Art Award competition in 1957.

BELOW: John Sloan's oil painting, *A Window on the Street* (1912), reflects his interest in the same theme that fascinated Hopper: solitary introspection.

Hopper liked to drive: in 1927 the couple bought their first automobile, a secondhand Dodge. Always economically minded, the Hoppers made a practice of buying only secondhand cars, and then driving them until they literally fell to pieces. As a response to the new freedom offered by the automobile to America and to Hopper personally, highways and gas stations appear as the subjects of many of his paintings, including *Gas* (1940), *Route Six, Eastham* (1941), *Solitude* (1944), *Four Lane Road* (1956), and even *Western Motel* (1957), where a car is clearly visible through the motel window.

LEFT: Edward Hopper pictured at the age of 73, apparently as lost in thought as many of the subjects of his paintings.

RIGHT: A contemporary scene from *Carousel*; Hopper and Jo were regular theatergoers, and theatrical settings often found their way into Hopper's work.

Even after having achieved artistic success and financial independence, Hopper and his wife chose to remain in the walk-up apartment building in Washington Square. Jo, in fact, encouraged her husband's thrift: she shopped for their clothes at Woolworth's, and they wore them until they were threadbare. They both preferred to live in somewhat bare, unembellished surroundings, whether in New York or at the summer home in Cape Cod that the couple had bought in 1934. Their only extravagances were the purchase of books and frequent trips to the theater, movies and restaurants (Jo, it seems, was not too keen on domestic duties such as cooking). Early in his youth, Hopper had sketched people in restaurants, and after he returned from Paris he painted *Le Bistro*; as an illustrator he also produced restaurant and café scenes. The first restaurant painting of Hopper's mature phase was *New York Restaurant* (c. 1922). Through a variety of compositions, Hopper went on to develop the theme in which the restaurant was the setting for the often solitary, introspective figures he favored. In *Automat* (1927), a young woman is sitting thoughtfully over her coffee cup; in *Chop Suey* (1929), two women are engrossed in their quiet conversation; *Tables for Ladies* (1930) puts the isolated individual nature of the cashier and waitress in the foreground; while in *Sunlight in a Cafeteria* (1958), Hopper uses the restaurant as the setting in which to depict the tensions between the male and female customers, who are aware of each other's presence, but appear not to have acknowledged the fact to each other.

Both Hopper and his wife adored the theater and movies, and their frequent outings affected Hopper's paintings in two ways: firstly, in his choice of theaters and movie houses as subject matter and, secondly, in his development of compositions that were often influenced by set designs, and by cinematic devices such as cropping or unusual angles of vision. *Two on the Aisle* (1927) was Hopper's first important painting of a theater scene, while the later painting, *First Row Orchestra* (1951), depicts the similar theme of a stylish couple seated near the stage before the start of the performance. One of Hopper's most surprising theatrical paintings, *Girlie Show* (1941), depicts a nude burlesque dancer. However, such overt sexuality is unique in his work. The significance of theatrical themes for Hopper is emphasized by two of the last four paintings completed before his death in 1967. In *Intermission* (1963), Hopper again presents a solitary figure seated calmly, as if awaiting the return of her companions before the play recommences. Two years later, in 1965, Hopper painted *Two Comedians*. Jo was later to confirm that the two figures on stage represented her and her husband. Hopper was aware of his impending death – he had been ill for some time – and in *Two Comedians* he symbolized his passing by creating a farewell picture in which he and his wife "bow out" from their performance together. In the picture, the tall male figure on the stage bows to the applause of the unseen audience, while the female figure stands a step behind and gestures to her partner.

Two years after completing *Two Comedians*, Edward Hopper died. A year later Jo, who herself had never stopped painting, but who also devoted most of her energy to protecting the privacy that she and her husband so jealously guarded, also died.

Après-Midi de Juin or **_L'Après-Midi de Printemps,_**
1907
Oil on canvas, 23½ × 28½ in.
Josephine N. Hopper Bequest,
Collection of the Whitney Museum of American Art,
New York, NY
(70.1172)

Le Quai des Grands Augustins with Tree, 1907
Oil on canvas, 23¾ × 28¾ in.
Josephine N. Hopper Bequest,
Collection of the Whitney Museum of American Art,
New York, NY
(70.1226)

Railroad Train, 1908
Oil on canvas, 24 × 29 in.
Gift of Fred T. Murphy, Esq.,
© Addison Gallery of American Art,
Phillips Academy, Andover, MA
(1944.10)

Summer Interior, 1909
Oil on canvas, 24 × 29 in.
Josephine N. Hopper Bequest,
Collection of the Whitney Museum of American Art,
New York, NY
(70.1197)

ABOVE:
The Louvre in a Thunderstorm, 1909
Oil on canvas, 23 × 28¾ in.
Bequest of Josephine N. Hopper,
Collection of the Whitney Museum of American Art,
New York, NY
(70.1223)

RIGHT:
Italian Quarter, Gloucester, 1912
Oil on canvas, 23⅜ × 28½ in.
Josephine N. Hopper Bequest,
Collection of the Whitney Museum of American Art,
New York, NY
(70.1214)

The Dories, Ogunquit, 1914
Oil on canvas, 24 × 29 in.
Josephine N. Hopper Bequest,
Collection of the Whitney Museum of American Art,
New York, NY
(70.1196)

Apartment Houses, *c.* 1924
Oil on canvas, 24 × 28$^{15}/_{16}$ in.
John Lambert Fund,
The Pennsylvania Academy of the Fine Arts,
Philadelphia, PA
(1925.5)

New York Pavements, 1924
Oil on canvas, 24 × 29 in.
Gift of Walter P. Chrysler, Jr.,
The Chrysler Museum, Norfolk, VA
(83.591)

Skyline Near Washington Square, 1925
Watercolor on cardboard, 15¹⁄₁₆ × 21⁹⁄₁₆ in.
Edward W. Root Bequest,
Munson-Williams-Proctor Institute,
Museum of Art, Utica, NY
(57.161)

Self-Portrait, 1925-30
Oil on canvas, 25 1/16 × 20 3/8 in.
Bequest of Josephine N. Hopper,
Collection of the Whitney Museum of American Art,
New York, NY
(70.1165)

Sunday, 1926
Oil on canvas, 29 × 34 in.
The Phillips Collection, Washington, D.C.

Eleven A.M., 1926
Oil on canvas, 28⅛ × 36⅛ in.
Gift of the Joseph H. Hirshhorn Foundation, 1966,
Hirshhorn Museum and Sculpture Garden,
Smithsonian Institution, Washington, D.C.
(66.2504)

Bow of Beam Trawler Osprey, 1926
Watercolor over charcoal on paper, 14 × 20 in.
Gift of Mr. and Mrs. G. Gordon Hertslet,
The Saint Louis Art Museum, MO
(1:1972)

Captain Strout's House, Portland Head, 1927
Watercolor on paper, 14 × 20 in.
The Ella Gallup Sumner and Mary Catlin Sumner Fund,
Wadsworth Atheneum, Hartford, CT
(1928.3)

Custom House, Portland, Maine, 1927
Watercolor on paper, 14 × 20 in.
Gift of Robert W. Huntingdon,
Wadsworth Atheneum, Hartford, CT
(1946.232)

Lighthouse and Buildings, Portland Head, Cape Elizabeth, 1927
Watercolor on paper, 13½ × 19½ in.
Bequest of John T. Spaulding,
Courtesy, Museum of Fine Arts, Boston, MA
(48.723)

The City, 1927
Oil on canvas, 27½ × 37 in.
Gift of C. Leonard Pfeiffer,
Collection of the University of Arizona,
Museum of Art, Tucson, AZ
(X45.9.23)

Two on the Aisle, 1927
Oil on canvas, 40⅛ × 48¼ in.
Purchased with funds from the Libbey Endowment,
Gift of Edward Drummond Libbey,
The Toledo Museum of Art, Toledo, OH
(1935.49)

Lighthouse Hill, 1927
Oil on canvas, 28¼ × 39½ in.
Gift of Mr. and Mrs. Maurice Purnell,
Dallas Museum of Art, TX
(1958.9)

Drug Store, 1927
Oil on canvas, 29 × 40 in.
Bequest of John T. Spaulding,
Courtesy, Museum of Fine Arts, Boston, MA
(48.564)

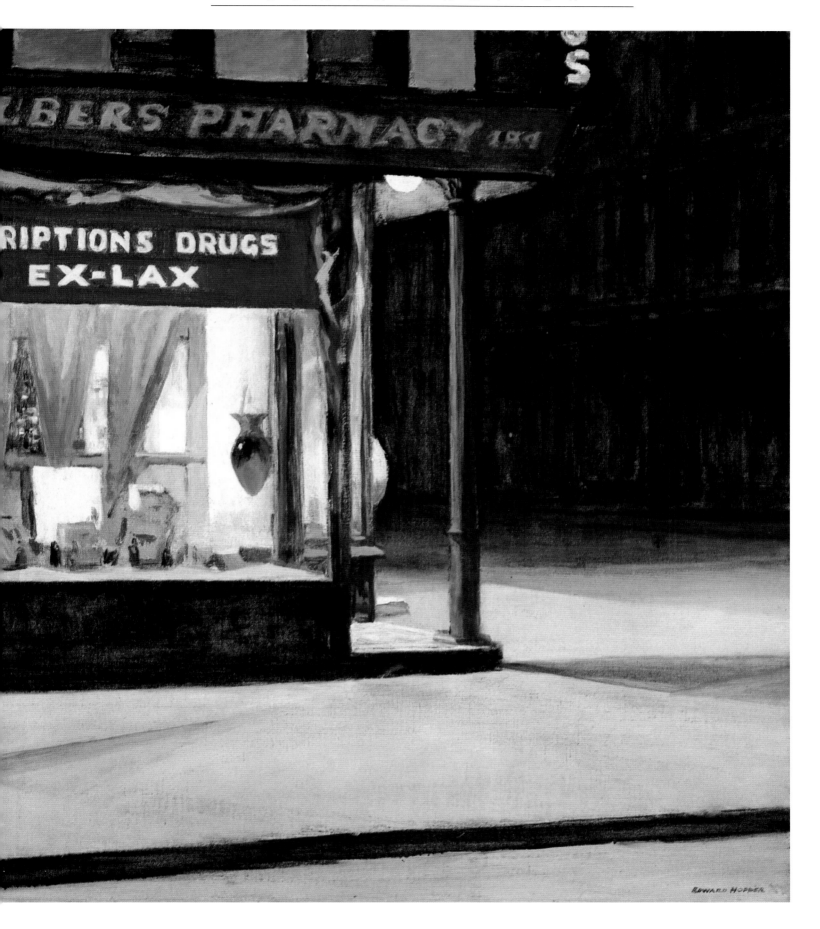

Automat, 1927
Oil on canvas, 28⅛ × 36 in.
Des Moines Art Center,
Permanent Collection, IA
(1958:2)

From Williamsburg Bridge, 1928
Oil on canvas, 29 × 43 in.
George A. Hearn Fund, 1937,
The Metropolitan Museum of Art,
New York, NY
(37.44)

Adam's House, 1928
Watercolor on paper, 16 × 25 in.
The Roland P. Murdock Collection,
Wichita Art Museum, KS
(M122.54)

49

**Freight Cars,
Gloucester,**
1928
Oil on canvas, 29⅛ × 40¼ in.
Gift of Edward W. Root, in
recognition of the 25th
Anniversary,
© Addison Gallery of
American Art,
Phillips Academy,
Andover, MA
(1956.7)

PAGES 52-53: **The Lighthouse at Two Lights,** 1929
Oil on canvas, 29½ × 43¼ in.
Hugo Kastor Fund, 1962,
The Metropolitan Museum of Art, New York, NY
(62.95)

Chop Suey, 1929
Oil on canvas, 32 × 38 in.
Mr. and Mrs. Barney A. Ebsworth

OPPOSITE PAGE:
Methodist Church, Provincetown, 1930
Watercolor on paper, 25 × 19¾ in.
The Ella Gallup Sumner and Mary Catlin Sumner Fund,
Wadsworth Atheneum, Hartford, CT
(1951.19)

Highland Light (North Truro), 1930
Watercolor over graphite on white paper, 16½ × 25¾ in.
Louise E. Bettens Fund,
Courtesy of the Fogg Art Museum,
Harvard University Art Museums, Cambridge, MA
(1930.462)

Tables for Ladies, 1930
Oil on canvas, 48¼ × 60¼ in.
George A. Hearn Fund, 1931,
The Metropolitan Museum of Art, New York, NY
(31.62)

Early Sunday Morning, 1930
Oil on canvas, 35 × 60 in.
Purchase, with Funds from Gertrude Vanderbilt Whitney,
Collection of the Whitney Museum of American Art,
New York, NY
(31.426)

Hills, South Truro, 1930
Oil on canvas, 27³⁄₁₆ × 43⅛ in.
Hinman B. Hurlbut Collection,
© The Cleveland Museum of Art, OH
(2647.31)

High Road, 1931
Watercolor on paper, 20 × 28 in.
Josephine N. Hopper Bequest,
Collection of the Whitney Museum of American Art,
New York, NY
(70.1163)

New York, New Haven and Hartford, 1931
Oil on canvas, 32 × 50 in.
Emma Harter Sweetser,
© 1989 Indianapolis Museum of Art, IN
(32.177)

Barber Shop, 1931
Oil on canvas, 60 × 78 in.
Gift of Roy R. Neuberger,
Collection Neuberger Museum of Art,
Purchase College, State University of New York, Purchase, NY
(76.26.54)

Marshall's House, 1932
Watercolor on paper, 14 × 20 in.
Gift of Henry and Walter Keney,
Wadsworth Atheneum, Hartford, CT
(1933.93)

November, Washington Square,
begun *c.* 1932, completed 1959
Oil on canvas, 34⅛ × 50¼ in.
Gift of Mrs. Sterling Morton
for the Preston Morton Collection,
Santa Barbara Museum of Art, CA
(1960.64)

Room in New York, 1932
Oil on canvas, 29 × 36 in.
UNL-F. M. Hall Collection,
Sheldon Memorial Art Gallery,
University of Nebraska, Lincoln, NE
(1936.H-166)

Room in Brooklyn, 1932
Oil on canvas, 29 × 34 in.
Charles Henry Hayden Fund,
Courtesy, Museum of Fine Arts, Boston, MA
(35.66)

Ryder's House, 1933
Oil on canvas, 38⅛ × 50 in.
National Museum of American Art,
Washington, D.C./Art Resource, NY
(1981.76)

East Wind over Weehawken, 1934
Oil on canvas, 34 × 50¼ in.
Collections Fund,
The Pennsylvania Academy of the Fine Arts,
Philadelphia, PA
(1952.12)

Macomb's Dam Bridge, 1935
Oil on canvas, 35 × 60³⁄₁₆ in.
Bequest of Miss Mary T. Crockcroft,
The Brooklyn Museum, NY
(57.145)

OVERLEAF: **Yawl Riding a Swell,** 1935
Watercolor over graphite on off-white wove paper,
19⅞ × 27¾ in.
Worcester Art Museum, MA
(1935.145)

House at Dusk, 1935
Oil on canvas, 36½ × 50 in.
The John Barton Payne Fund,
Virginia Museum of Fine Arts, Richmond, VA
(53.8)

Jo Painting, 1936
Oil on canvas, 18 × 16 in.
Josephine N. Hopper Bequest,
Collection of the Whitney Museum of American Art,
New York, NY
(70.1171)

Five A.M., *c.* 1937
Oil on canvas, 25 × 36 in.
The Roland P. Murdock Collection,
Wichita Art Museum, KS
(M4.39)

Compartment C, Car 293, 1938
Oil on canvas, 20 × 19 in.
Collection of I.B.M. Corporation, Armonk, NY

Pretty Penny, 1939
Oil on canvas, 29 × 40 in.
Gift of Mrs. Charles MacArthur (Helen Hayes '40), 1965,
Smith College Museum of Art, Northampton, MA
(1965:4)

Ground Swell, 1939
Oil on canvas, 36½ × 50¼ in.
Museum Purchase, William A. Clark Fund,
In the Collection of The Corcoran Gallery of Art,
Washington, D.C.
(43.6)

Cape Cod Evening, 1939
Oil on canvas, 30¼ × 40¼ in.
John Hay Whitney Collection,
© 1994 Board of Trustees,
National Gallery of Art, Washington, D.C.
(1982.76.6)

Bridle Path, 1939
Oil on canvas, 28⅜ × 42⅛ in.
Anonymous Gift,
San Francisco Museum of Modern Art, CA
(76.174)

Street Scene, Gloucester, *c.* 1940
Oil on canvas, 28 × 36¼ in.
The Edwin and Virginia Irwin Memorial,
Cincinnati Art Museum, OH
(1959.49)

Office at Night, 1940
Oil on canvas, 22³⁄₁₆ × 25⅛ in.
Gift of T. B. Walker Acquisition Fund,
Gilbert M. Walker Fund, 1948,
Collection Walker Art Center, Minneapolis, MN
(48.21)

Route Six, Eastham, 1941
Oil on canvas, 27½ × 38¼ in.
Sheldon Swope Art Museum, Terre Haute, IN
(42.01)

Nighthawks, 1942
Oil on canvas, 30 × 56¾ in.
Friends of American Art Collection,
© 1994 The Art Institute of Chicago, IL
(1942.51)

Hotel Lobby, 1943
Oil on canvas, 32¼ × 40¾ in.
William Ray Adams Memorial Collection,
© 1989 Indianapolis Museum of Art, IN
(47.4)

Summertime, 1943
Oil on canvas, 29¹⁄₁₆ × 44 in.
Gift of Dora Sexton Brown,
Delaware Art Museum, Wilmington, DE
(62.28)

August in the City, 1945
Oil on canvas, 23 × 30 in.
Norton Gallery and School of Art,
West Palm Beach, FL
(Pl.258)

Rooms for Tourists, 1945
Oil on canvas, 30¼ × 42⅛ in.
Bequest of Stephen Carlton Clark,
Yale University Art Gallery, New Haven, CT
(1961.11.30)

Jo in Wyoming, 1946
Watercolor on paper, 13¹⁵⁄₁₆ × 20 in.
Bequest of Josephine N. Hopper,
Collection of the Whitney Museum of American Art,
New York, NY
(70.1159)

Approaching a City, 1946
Oil on canvas, 27⅛ × 36 in.
The Phillips Collection, Washington, D.C.

El Palacio, 1946
Watercolor on paper, 22⅜ × 30¾ in.
Exchange, Collection of the Whitney Museum of American Art,
New York, NY
(50.2)

Pennsylvania Coal Town, 1947
Oil on linen on canvas, 28 × 40 in.
The Butler Institute of American Art, Youngstown, OH
(948-0-115)

Seven A.M., 1948
Oil on canvas, 30 × 40 in.
Purchase and Exchange,
Collection of the Whitney Museum of American Art,
New York, NY
(50.8)

High Noon, 1949
Oil on canvas, 27½ × 39½ in.
Gift of Mr. and Mrs. Anthony Haswell,
The Dayton Art Institute, OH
(71.7)

Conference at Night, *c.* 1949
Oil on canvas, 27¾ × 40 in.
The Roland P. Murdock Collection,
Wichita Art Museum, KS
(M100.52)

Cape Cod Morning, 1950
Oil on canvas, 34¼ × 40⅛ in.
Gift of the Sara Roby Foundation,
National Museum of American Art,
Smithsonian Institution, Washington, D.C.
(1986.6.92)

Rooms by the Sea, 1951
Oil on canvas, 20 × 40⅛ in.
Bequest of Stephen Carlton Clark,
Yale University Art Gallery, New Haven, CT
(1961.18.29)

Morning Sun, 1952
Oil on canvas, 28⅛ × 40⅛ in
Museum Purchase – Howald Fund,
Columbus Museum of Art, OH
(54.31)

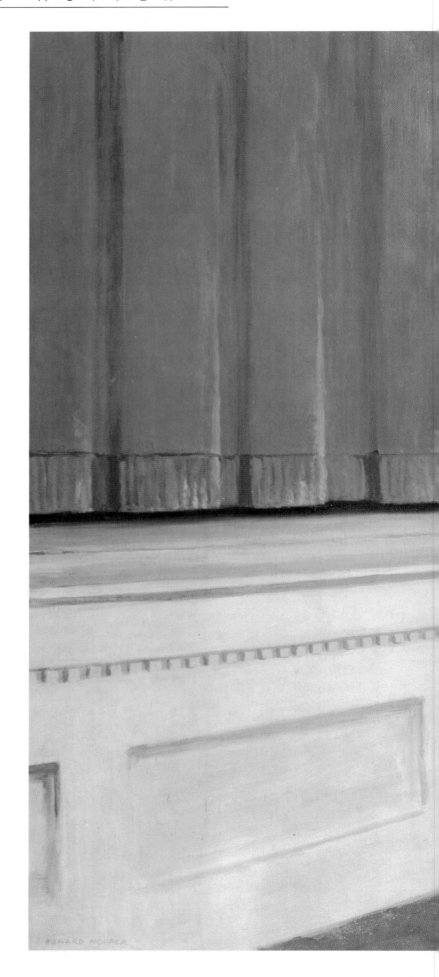

First Row Orchestra, 1951
Oil on canvas, 31⅛ × 40⅛ in.
Gift of Joseph H. Hirshhorn Foundation, 1966,
Hirshhorn Museum and Sculpture Garden,
Smithsonian Institution, Washington, D.C.
(66.2506)

112

Hotel by a Railroad, 1952
Oil on canvas, 31¼ × 40⅛ in.
Gift of the Joseph H. Hirshhorn Foundation, 1966,
Hirshhorn Museum and Sculpture Garden,
Smithsonian Institution, Washington, D.C.
(66.2507)

City Sunlight, 1954
Oil on canvas, 28¼ × 40¼ in.
Gift of Joseph H. Hirshhorn Foundation, 1966,
Hirshhorn Museum and Sculpture Garden,
Smithsonian Institution, Washington, D.C.
(66.2505)

Office in a Small City, 1953
Oil on canvas, 28 × 40 in.
George A. Hearn Fund, 1953,
The Metropolitan Museum of Art, New York, NY
(53.183)

South Carolina Morning, 1955
Oil on canvas, 30 × 40 in.
Given in memory of Otto L. Spaeth by his Family,
Collection of the Whitney Museum of American Art,
New York, NY
(67.13)

Sunlight on Brownstones, 1956
Oil on canvas, 29¾ × 39¾ in.
The Roland P. Murdock Collection,
Wichita Art Museum, KS
(M148.57)

Western Motel, 1957
Oil on canvas, 30¼ × 50⅛ in.
Bequest of Stephen Carlton Clark,
Yale University Art Gallery, New Haven, CT
(1961.18.32)

Sunlight in a Cafeteria, 1958
Oil on canvas, 40¼ × 60⅛ in.
Bequest of Stephen Carlton Clark,
Yale University Art Gallery, New Haven, CT
(1961.18.31)

People in the Sun, 1960
Oil on canvas, 40⅜ × 60⅜ in.
Gift of S. C. Johnson & Son, Inc.,
National Museum of American Art,
Smithsonian Institution, Washington, D.C.
(1969.47.61)

ABOVE:
Second Story Sunlight, 1960
Oil on canvas, 40 × 50 in.
Purchase, with Funds from the Friends of the
Whitney Museum of American Art,
Collection of the Whitney Museum of American Art,
New York, NY
(60.54)

OVERLEAF:
A Woman in the Sun, 1961
Oil on canvas, 40 × 60 in.
50th Anniversary Gift of Mr. and Mrs. Albert Hackett
in Honor of Edith and Lloyd Goodrich,
Collection of the Whitney Museum of American Art,
New York, NY
(84.31)

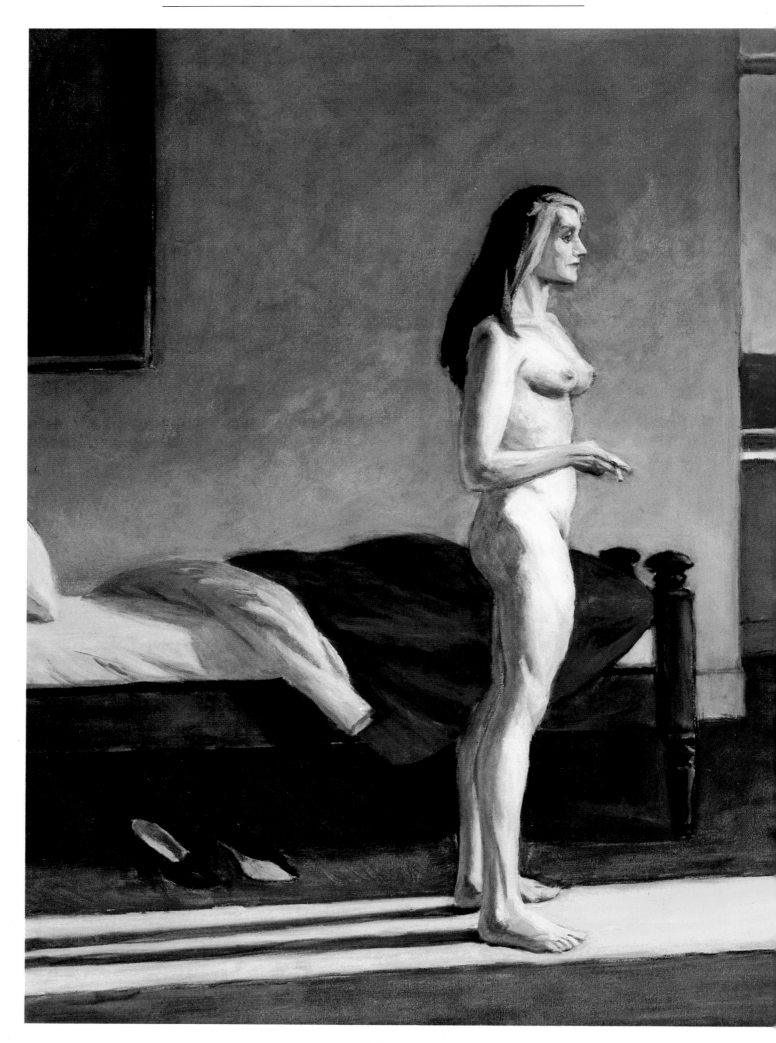